The Poetry of Bliss Carman

Volume IX - Ballads and Lyrics

William Bliss Carman was born in Fredericton, in New Brunswick on April 15th 1861. He was educated at Fredericton Collegiate School before moving to the University of New Brunswick, obtaining his B.A. there in 1881. As is common with so many writers his first published piece was for the University magazine and for Carman that was in 1879.

After several years editing various magazines and periodicals Carman first published a poetry volume in 1893 with Low Tide on Grand Pré. There was no Canadian company prepared to publish and when an American company did so it went bankrupt.

The following year was decidedly better. His partnership with the American poet Richard Hovey had given birth to Songs of Vagabondia. It was an immediate success.

That success prompted the Boston firm, Stone & Kimball, to reissue Low Tide on Grand Pré and to hire Carman as the editor of its literary journal, The Chapbook.

Carman brought out, in 1895, Behind the Arras, a somewhat more serious and philosophical work centered on the premise of a long meditation, using the speaker's house and its many rooms, as a symbol of life and the choices to be made.

In 1896 Carman met Mrs Mary Perry King, who rapidly became patron, adviser and sometime lover. She also became his writing collaborator on two verse dramas.

In 1897 Carman published Ballad of Lost Haven, and in 1898, By the Aurelian Wall, the title poem itself was an elegy to John Keats and the book was a collection of formal elegies.

As the century turned Carman was hard at work on a five-volume set of poetry "Pans Pipes". The excellence of a number of these poems did much to install Carman as the most noted of Canadian Poets and eventually their own Poet Laureate.

In 1912 the final work in the Vagabondia series was published. Richard Hovey had died in 1900 and so this last work was purely Carman's. It has a distinct elegiac tone as if remembering the past works themselves.

On October 28th, 1921 Carman was honored by the newly-formed Canadian Authors' Association where he was crowned Canada's Poet Laureate with a wreath of maple leaves.

William Bliss Carman died of a brain hemorrhage at the age of 68 in New Canaan on the 8th June, 1929.

Index of Contents

THE NANCY'S PRIDE

On the long slow heave of a lazy sea,
To the flap of an idle sail,
The Nancy's Pride went out on the tide;
And the skipper stood by the rail.

All down, all down by the sleepy town,
With the hollyhocks a-row
In the little poppy gardens,
The sea had her in tow.

They let her slip by the breathing rip,
Where the bell is never still,

And over the sounding harbour bar,
And under the harbour hill.

She melted into the dreaming noon,
Out of the drowsy land,
In sight of a flag of goldy hair,
To the kiss of a girlish hand.

For the lass who hailed the lad who sailed,
Was —who but his April bride?
And of all the fleet of Grand Latite,
Her pride was the Nancy's Pride.

So the little vessel faded down
With her creaking boom a-swing,
Till a wind from the deep came up with a creep,
And caught her wing and wing.

She made for the lost horizon line,
Where the clouds a-castled lay,
While the boil and seethe of the open sea
Hung on her frothing way.

She lifted her hull like a breasting gull
Where the rolling valleys be,
And dipped where the shining porpoises
Put ploughshares through the sea.

A fading sail on the far sea-line,
About the turn of the tide,
As she made for the Banks on her maiden cruise
Was the last of the Nancy's Pride.

To-day a boy with goldy hair,
In a garden of Grand Latite,
From his mother's knee looks out to sea
For the coming of the fleet.

They all may home on a sleepy tide,
To the flap of the idle sail;
But it's never again the Nancy's Pride
That answers a human hail.
They all may home on a sleepy tide
To the sag of an idle sheet;
But it's never again the Nancy's Pride
That draws men down the street.

On the Banks to-night a fearsome sight

The fishermen behold,
Keeping the ghost-watch in the moon
When the small hours are cold.

When the light wind veers, and the white fog clears,
They see by the after rail
An unknown schooner creeping up
With mildewed spar and sail.

Her crew lean forth by the rotting shrouds,
With the Judgment in their face;
And to their mates' 'God save you!'
Have never a word of grace.

Then into the gray they sheer away,
On the awful polar tide;
And the sailors know they have seen the wraith
Of the missing Nancy's Pride.

THE GRAVEDIGGER

Oh, the shambling sea is a sexton old,
And well his work is done.
With an equal grave for lord and knave,
He buries them every one.

Then hoy and rip, with a rolling hip,
He makes for the nearest shore;
And God, who sent him a thousand ship,
Will send him a thousand more;
But some he'll save for a bleaching grave,
And shoulder them in to shore,—
Shoulder them in, shoulder them in,
Shoulder them in to shore.

Oh, the ships of Greece and the ships of Tyre
Went out, and where are they?
In the port they made, they are delayed
With the ships of yesterday.

He followed the ships of England far,
As the ships of long ago;
And the ships of France they led him a dance,
But he laid them all arow.

Oh, a loafing, idle lubber to him

Is the sexton of the town;
For sure and swift, with a guiding lift,
He shovels the dead men down.

But though he delves so fierce and grim,
His honest graves are wide,
As well they know who sleep below
The dredge of the deepest tide.

Oh, he works with a rollicking stave at lip,
And loud is the chorus skirled;
With the burly rote of his rumbling throat
He batters it down the world.

He learned it once in his father's house,
Where the ballads of old were sung;
And merry enough is the burden rough,
But no man knows the tongue.

Oh, fair, they say, was his bride to see,
And wilful she must have been,
That she could bide at his gruesome side
When the first red dawn came in.

And sweet, they say, is her kiss to those
She greets to his border home;
And softer than sleep her hand's first sweep
That beckons, and they come.

Oh, crooked is he, but strong enough
To handle the tallest mast;
From the royal barque to the slaver dark,
He buries them all at last.

Then hoy and rip, with a rolling hip,
He makes for the nearest shore;
And God, who sent him a thousand ship,
Will send him a thousand more;

But some he'll save for a bleaching grave,
And shoulder them in to shore,—
Shoulder them in, shoulder them in,
Shoulder them in to shore

A MORE ANCIENT MARINER

The swarthy bee is a buccaneer,
A burly, velveted rover,
Who loves the booming wind in his ear
As he sails the seas of clover.

A waif of the goblin pirate crew,
With not a soul to deplore him,
He steers for the open verge of blue
With the filmy world before him.

Out in the day, haphazard, alone,
Booms the old vagrant hummer,
With only his whim to pilot him
Through the splendid vast of summer.

His flimsy sails abroad on the wind
Are shivered with fairy thunder;
On a line that sings to the light of his wings
He makes for the lands of wonder.

He harries the ports of the Hollyhocks,
And levies on poor Sweetbrier;
He drinks the whitest wine of Phlox,
And the Rose is his desire.

He hangs in the Willows a night and a day;
He rifles the Buckwheat patches;
Then battens his store of pelf galore
Under the tautest hatches.

He woos the Poppy and weds the Peach,
Inveigles Daffodilly,
And then like a tramp abandons each
For the gorgeous Canada Lily.

There's not a soul in the garden world
But wishes the day were shorter,
When Mariner B. puts out to sea
With the wind in the proper quarter.

Or, so they say! But I have my doubts;
For the flowers are only human,
And the valour and gold of a vagrant bold
Were always dear to woman.

He dares to boast, along the coast,
The beauty of Highland Heather,—
How he and she, with night on the sea,

Lay out on the hills together.

His morals are mixed, but his will is fixed;
He prospers after his kind,
And follows an instinct, compass-sure,
The philosophers call blind.

And that is why, when he comes to die,
He'll have an easier sentence
Than some one I know who thinks just so,
And then leaves room for repentance.

SPRING SONG

Make me over, mother April,
When the sap begins to stir!
When thy flowery hand delivers
All the mountain-prisoned rivers,
And thy great heart beats and quivers
To revive the days that were,
Make me over, mother April,
When the sap begins to stir!

Take my dust and all my dreaming,
Count my heart-beats one by one,
Send them where the winters perish;
Then some golden noon re-cherish
And restore them in the sun,
Flower and scent and dust and dreaming,
With their heart-beats every one!

Make me of thy seed to-morrow,
When the sap begins to stir!
Tawny light-foot, sleepy bruin,
Bright-eyes in the orchard ruin,
Gnarl the good life goes askew in,
Whisky-jack, or tanager,—
Make me anything to-morrow,
When the sap begins to stir!

Make me even (How do I know?)
Like my friend the gargoyle there;
It may be the heart within him
Swells that doltish hands should pin him
Fixed for ever in mid-air.
Make me even sport for swallows,

Like the soaring gargoyle there!

Give me the old clue to follow,
Through the labyrinth of night!
Clod of clay with heart of fire,
Things that burrow and aspire,
With the vanishing desire,
For the perishing delight,—
Only the old clue to follow,
Through the labyrinth of night!

Make me over, mother April,
When the sap begins to stir!
Fashion me from swamp or meadow,
Garden plot or ferny shadow,
Hyacinth or humble burr!
Make me over, mother April,
When the sap begins to stir!

Make me over in the morning
From the rag-bag of the world!
Scraps of dream and duds of daring,
Home-brought stuff from far sea-faring,
Faded colours once so flaring,
Shreds of banners long since furled!
Hues of ash and glints of glory,
In tim rag-bag of the world!

Let me taste the old immortal
Indolence of life once more;
Not recalling nor foreseeing,
Let the great slow joys of being
Well my heart through as of yore!
Let me taste the old immortal
Indolence of life once more!

Give me the old drink for rapture,
The delirium to drain,
All my fellows drank in plenty
At the Three Score Inns and Twenty
From the mountains to the main!
Give me the old drink for rapture,
The delirium to drain!

Only make me over, April,
When the sap begins to stir!
Make me man or make me woman,
Make me oaf or ape or human,

Cup of flower or cone of fir;
Make me anything but neuter
When the sap begins to stir!

Now the joys of the road are chiefly these:
A crimson touch on the hard-wood trees;
A vagrant's morning wide and blue,
In early fall, when the wind walks, too;
A shadowy highway cool and brown,
Alluring up and enticing down
From rippled water to dappled swamp,
From purple glory to scarlet pomp;
The outward eye, the quiet will,
And the striding heart from hill to hill;
The tempter apple over the fence;
The cobweb bloom on the yellow quince;
The palish asters along the wood,—
A lyric touch of the solitude;
An open hand, an easy shoe,
And a hope to make the day go through,—
Another to sleep with, and a third
To wake me up at the voice of a bird;

A scrap of gossip at the ferry;
A comrade neither glum nor merry,
Who never defers and never demands,
But, smiling, takes the world in his hands,—
Seeing it good as when God first saw
And gave it the weight of his will for law.
And O the joy that is never won,
But follows and follows the journeying sun,
By marsh and tide, by meadow and stream,
A will-o'-the-wind, a light-o'-dream,
The racy smell of the forest loam,
When the stealthy, sad-heart leaves go home;
The broad gold wake of the afternoon;
The silent fleck of the cold new moon;
The sound of the hollow sea's release
Front stormy tumult to starry peace;
With only another league to wend;
And two brown arms at the journey's end!
These are the joys of the open road—
For him who travels without a load.

THE MENDICANTS

We are as mendicants who wait
Along the roadside in the sun.
Tatters of yesterday and shreds
Of morrow clothe us every one.

And some are dotards, who believe
And glory in the days of old;
While some are dreamers, harping still
Upon an unknown age of gold.

Hopeless or witless! Not one heeds,
As lavish Time comes down the way
And tosses in the suppliant hat
One great new-minted gold To-day.

Ungrateful heart and grudging thanks,
His beggar's wisdom only sees
Housing and bread and beer enough;
He knows no other things than these.

O foolish ones, put by your care!
Where wants are many, joys are few;
And at the wilding springs of peace,
God keeps an open house for you.

But that some Fortunatus' gift
Is lying there within his hand,
More costly than a pot of pearls,
His dulness does not understand.

And so his creature heart is filled;
His shrunken self goes starved away.
Let him wear brand-new garments still,
Who has a threadbare soul, I say.

But there be others, happier few,
The vagabondish sons of God,
Who know the by-ways and the flowers,
And care not how the world may plod.

They idle down the traffic lands,
And loiter through the woods with spring;
To them the glory of the earth
Is but to hear a bluebird sing.

They too receive each one his Day;
But their wise heart knows many things
Beyond the sating of desire,
Above the dignity of kings.

One I remember kept his coin,
And laughing flipped it in the air;
But when two strolling pipe-players
Came by, he tossed it to the pair.

Spendthrift of joy, his childish heart
Danced to their wild outlandish bars;
Then supperless he laid him down
That night, and slept beneath the stars.

THE FAITHLESS LOVER

I.

O Life, dear Life, in this fair house
Long since did I, it seems to me,
In some mysterious doleful way
Fall out of love with thee.

For, Life, thou art become a ghost,
A memory of days gone by,
A poor forsaken thing between
A heartache and a sigh.

And now, with shadows from the hills
Thronging the twilight, wraith on wraith,
Unlock the door and let me go
To thy dark rival Death!

II.

O Heart, dear Heart, in this fair house
Why hast thou wearied and grown tired,
Between a morning and a night,
Of all thy soul desired?

Fond one, who cannot understand,
Even these shadows on the floor,
Yet must be dreaming of dark loves

And joys beyond my door!

But I am beautiful past all
The timid tumult of thy mood,
And thou returning not must still
Be mine in solitude.

IN THE WINGS

The play is Life; and this round earth
The narrow stage whereon
We act before an audience
Of actors dead and gone.

There is a figure in the wings
That never goes away,
And though I cannot see his face,
I shudder while I play.

His shadow looms behind me here,
Or capers at my side;
And when I mouth my lines in dread,
Those scornful lips deride.

Sometimes a hooting laugh breaks out,
And startles me alone;
While all my fellows, wondering
At my stage-fright, play on.

I fear that when my Exit comes,
I shall encounter there,
Stronger than fate, or time, or love
And sterner than despair,

The Final Critic of the craft,
As stage tradition tells;
And yet—perhaps 'twill only be
The jester with his bells.

HACK AND HEW

Hack and Hew were the sons of God
In the earlier earth than now;
One at his right hand, one at his left,

To obey as he taught them how.

And Hack was blind and Hew was dumb,
But both had the wild, wild heart;
And God's calm will was their burning will,
And the gist of their toil was art.

They made the moon and the belted stars,
They set the sun to ride;
They loosed the girdle and veil of the sea,
The wind and the purple tide.

Both flower and beast beneath their hands
To beauty and speed outgrew,—
The furious fumbling hand of Hack,
And the glorying hand of Hew.

Then, fire and clay, they fashioned a man,
And painted him rosy brown;
And God himself blew hard in his eyes:
'Let them burn till they smoulder down!'

And 'There!' said Hack, and 'There!' thought Hew,
'We'll rest, for our toil is done.'
But 'Nay,' the Master Workman said,
'For your toil is just begun.

'And ye who served me of old as God
Shall serve me anew as man,
Till I compass the dream that is in my heart,
And perfect the vaster plan.'

And still the craftsman over his craft,
In the vague white light of dawn,
With God's calm will for his burning will,
While the mounting day comes on,

Yearning, wind-swift, indolent, wild,
Toils with those shadowy two,—
The faltering restless hand of Hack
And the tireless hand of Hew.

HEM AND HAW

Hem and Haw were the sons of sin,
Created to shally and shirk;

Hem lay 'round and Haw looked on
While God did all the work.

Hem was a fogey, and Haw was a prig,
For both had the dull, dull mind;
And whenever they found a thing to do,
They yammered and went it blind.

Hem was the father of bigots and bores;
As the sands of the sea were they.
And Haw was the father of all the tribe
Who criticise to-day.

But God was an artist from the first,
And knew what he was about;
While over his shoulder sneered these two,
And advised him to rub it out.

They prophesied ruin ere man was made:
'Such folly must surely fail!'
And when he was done, 'Do you think, my Lord,
He's better without a tail?'

And still in the honest working world,
With posture and hint and smirk,
These sons of the devil are standing by
While Man does all the work.

They balk endeavour and baffle reform
In the sacred name of law;
And over the quavering voice of Hem
Is the droning voice of Haw.

THE DUSTMAN

'Dustman, dustman!'
Through the deserted square he cries,
And babies put their rosy fists
Into their eyes.

There's nothing out of No-man's-land
So drowsy since the world began,
As 'Dustman, dustman,
Dustman.'

He goes his village round at dusk

From door to door, from day to day;
And when the children hear his step
They stop their play.

'Dustman, dustman!'
Far up the street he is descried,
And soberly the twilight games
Are laid aside.

'Dustman, dustman!'
There, Drowsyhead, the old refrain,
'Dustman, dustman!
It goes again.

Dustman, dustman,
Hurry by and let me sleep.
When most I wish for you to come,
You always creep.

Dustman, dustman,
And when I want to play some more,
You never then are farther off
Than the next door.

'Dustman, dustman!'
He beckles down the echoing curb,
A step that neither hopes nor hates
Ever disturb.

'Dustman, dustman!'
He never varies from one pace,
And the monotony of time
Is in his face.

And some day, with more potent dust,
Brought from his home beyond the deep,
And gently scattered on our eyes,
We, too, shall sleep,—

Hearing the call we know so well
Fade softly out as it began,
'Dustman, dustman,
Dustman!'

THE SLEEPERS

The tall carnations crown the garden walks
Bowed on their stalks.

Said Jock-a-dreams to John-a-nods,
'What are the odds
That we shall wake up here within the sun,
When time is done,
And pick up all the treasures one by one
Our hands let fall in sleep?' 'You have begun
To mutter in your dreams,'
Said John-a-nods to Jock-a-dreams,
And they both slept again.

The tall carnations in the sunset glow
Burned row on row.

Said John-a-nods to Jock-a-dreams,
'To me it seems
A thousand years since last you stirred and spoke,
And I awoke.
Was that the wind then trying to provoke
His brothers in their blessed sleep?' 'They choke,
Who mutter in their nods,'
Said Jock-a-dreams to John-a-nods.
And they both slept again.

The tall carnations only heard a sigh
Of dusk go by.

A CAPTAIN OF THE PRESS GANG

Shipmate, leave the ghostly shadows,
Where thy boon companions throng!
We will put to sea together
Through the twilight with a song.

Leering closer, rank and girding,
In this Black Port where we bide,
Reel a thousand flaring faces;
But escape is on the tide.

Let the tap-rooms of the city
Reek till the red dawn comes round.
There is better wine in plenty
On the cruise where we are bound.

I've aboard a hundred messmates
Better than these 'long-shore knaves.
There is wreckage on the shallows;
It's the open sea that saves.

Hark, lad, dost not hear it calling?
That's the voice thy father knew,
When he took the King's good cutlass
In his grip, and fought it through.

Who would palter at press-money
When he heard that sea-cry vast?
That's the call makes lords of lubbers,
When they ship before the mast.

Let thy cronies of the tavern
Keep their kisses bought with gold;
On the high seas there are regions
Where the heart is never old,

Where the great winds every morning
Sweep the sea-floor clean and white,
And upon the steel-blue arches
Burnish the great stars of night;

There the open hand will lose not,
Nor the loosened tongue betray.
Signed, and with our sailing orders,
We will clear before the day;

On the shining yards of heaven
See a wider dawn unfurled. . . .
The eternal slaves of beauty
Are the masters of the world.

IN THE WORKSHOP

Once in the Workshop, ages ago,
The clay was wet and the fire was low.

And He who was bent on fashioning man
Moulded a shape from a clod,
And put the loyal heart therein;
While another stood watching by.

'What's that?' said Beelzebub.

'A lover,' said God.
And Beelzebub frowned, for he knew that kind.

And then God fashioned a fellow shape
As lithe as a willow rod,
And gave it the merry roving eye
And the range of the open road.

'What's that?' said Beelzebub.
'A vagrant,' said God.
And Beelzebub smiled, for he knew that kind.

And last of all God fashioned a form,
And gave it, what was odd,
The loyal heart, and the roving eye;
And he whistled, light of care.

'What's that?' said Beelzebub.
'A poet,' said God.
And Beelzebub frowned, for he did not know.

IN THE HOUSE OF IDIEDAILY

Oh, but life went gaily, gaily,
In the house of Idiedaily!
There were always throats to sing
Down the river-banks with spring,
When the stir of heart's desire
Set the sapling's heart on fire.
Bobolincolns in the meadows,
Leisure in the purple shadows,
Till the poppies without number
Bowed their heads in crimson slumber,
And the twilight came to cover
Every un-reluctant lover.
Not a night but some brown maiden
Bettered all the dusk she strayed in,
While the roses in her hair
Bankrupted oblivion there.
Oh, but life went gaily, gaily,
In the house of Idiedaily!
But this hostelry, The Barrow,
With its chambers, bare and narrow,

Mean, ill-windowed, damp, and wormy,
Where the silence makes you squirmy,

And the guests are never seen to,
Is a vile place, a mere lean-to,
Not a traveller speaks well of,
Even worse than I heard tell of,
Mouldy, ramshackle, and foul—
What a dwelling for a soul!
Oh, but life went gaily, gaily,
In the house of Idiedaily!
There the hearth was always warm
From the slander of the storm.
There your comrade was your neighbour,
Living on to-morrow's labour.
And the board was always steaming,
Though Sir Ringlets might be dreaming.
Not a plate but scoffed at porridge,
Not a cup but floated borage.
There were always jugs of sherry
Waiting for the makers merry,
And the dark Burgundian wine
That would make a fool divine.
Oh, but life went gaily, gaily,
In the house of Idiedaily!

RESIGNATION

When I am only fit to go to bed,
Or hobble out to sit within the sun,
Ring down the curtain, say the play is done,
And the last petals of the poppy shed!

I do not want to live when I am old,
I have no use for things I cannot love;
And when the day that I am talking of
(Which God forfend!) is come, it will be cold.

But if there is another place than this,
Where all the men will greet me as 'Old Man,'
And all the women wrap me in a smile,
Where money is more useless than a kiss,
And good wine is not put beneath the ban,
I will go there and stay a little while.

IN A COPY OF BROWNING

Browning, old fellow,
Your leaves grow yellow,
Beginning to mellow
As seasons pass.
Your cover is wrinkled,
And stained and sprinkled,
And warped and crinkled
From sleep on the grass.

Is it a wine stain,
Or only a pine stain,
That makes such a fine stain
On your dull blue,—
Got as we numbered
The clouds that lumbered
Southward and slumbered
When day was through?

What is the dear mark
There like an earmark,
Only a tear mark
A woman let fall?—
As bending over
She bade me discover,
'Who plays the lover,
He loses all!'

With you for teacher
We learned love's feature
In every creature
That roves or grieves;
When winds were brawling,
Or bird-folk calling,
Or leaf-folk falling,
About our eaves.

No law must straiten
The ways they wait in,
Whose spirits greaten
And hearts aspire.
The world may dwindle,
And summer brindle,
So love but kindle
The soul to fire.

Here many a red line,
Or pencilled headline,
Shows love could wed line

To golden sense;
And something better
Than wisdom's fetter
Has made your letter
Dense to the dense.

No April robin,
Nor clacking bobbin,
Can make of Dobbin
A Pegasus;
But Nature's pleading
To man's unheeding,
Your subtile reading
Made clear to us.

You made us farers
And equal sharers
With homespun wearers
In home-made joys;
You made us princes
No plea convinces
That spirit winces
At dust and noise.

When Fate was nagging,
And days were dragging,
And fancy lagging,
You gave it scope,—
When eaves were drippy,
And pavements slippy,—
From Lippo Lippi
To Evelyn Hope.

When winter's arrow
Pierced to the marrow,
And thought was narrow,
You gave it room;
We guessed the warder
On Roland's border,
And helped to order
The Bishop's Tomb.

When winds were harshish,
And ways were marshish,
We found with Karshish
Escape at need;
Were bold with Waring
In far seafaring,

And strong in sharing
Ben Ezra's creed.

We felt the menace
Of lovers pen us,
Afloat in Venice
Devising fibs;
And little mattered
The rain that pattered,
While Blougram chattered
To Gigadibs.

And we too waited
With heart elated
And breathing bated,
For Pippa's song;
Saw Satan hover,
With wings to cover
Porphyria's lover,
Pompilia's wrong.

Long thoughts were started,
When youth departed
From the half-hearted
Riccardi's bride;
For, saith your fable,
Great Love is able
To slip the cable
And take the tide.

Or truth compels us
With Paracelsus,
Till nothing else is
Of worth at all.
Del Sarto's vision
Is our own mission,
And art's ambition
Is God's own call.

Through all the seasons,
You gave us reasons
For splendid treasons
To doubt and fear;
Bade no foot falter,
Though weaklings palter,
And friendships alter
From year to year.

Since first I sought you,
Found you and bought you,
Hugged you and brought you
Home from Cornhill,
While some upbraid you,
And some parade you,
Nine years have made you
My master still.

MR MOON: A SONG OF THE LITTLE PEOPLE

O Moon, Mr. Moon,
When you comin' down?
Down on the hilltop,
Down in the glen,
Out in the clearin',
To play with little men?
Moon, Mr. Moon,
When you comin' down?

O Mr. Moon,
Hurry up your stumps!
Don't you hear Bullfrog
Callin' to his wife,
And old black Cricket
A-wheezin' at his fife?
Hurry up your stumps,
And get on your pumps!
Moon, Mr. Moon,
When you comin' down?

O Mr. Moon,
Hurry up along!
The reeds in the current
Are whisperin' slow;
The river's a-wimplin'
To and fro.
Hurry up along,
Or you'll miss the song!
Moon, Mr. Moon,
When you comin' down?

O Mr. Moon,
We're all here!
Honey-bug, Thistledrift,
White-imp, Weird,

Wryface, Billiken,
Quidnunc, Queered;
We're all here,
And the coast is clear!
Moon, Mr. Moon,
When you comin' down?

O Mr. Moon,
We're the little men!
Dewlap, Pussymouse,
Ferntip, Freak,
Drink-again, Shambler,
Talkytalk, Squeak;
Three times ten
Of us little men!
Moon, Mr. Moon,
When you comin' down?

O Mr. Moon,
We're all ready!
Tallenough, Squaretoes,
Amble, Tip,
Buddybud, Heigho,
Little black Pip;
We're all ready,
And the wind walks steady!
Moon, Mr. Moon,
When you comin' down?

O Mr. Moon,
We're thirty score;
Yellowbeard, Piper,
Lieabed, Toots,
Meadowbee, Moonboy,
Bully-in-boots;
Three times more
Than thirty score.
Moon, Mr. Moon,
When you comin' down?

O Mr. Moon,
Keep your eye peeled;
Watch out to windward,
Or you'll miss the fun,
Down by the acre
Where the wheat-waves run;
Keep your eye peeled
For the open field.

Moon, Mr. Moon,
When you comin' down?

O Mr. Moon,
There's not much time!
Hurry, if you're comin',
You lazy old bones!
You can sleep to-morrow
While the Buzbuz drones;
There's not much time
Till the church-bells chime.
Moon, Mr. Moon,
When you comin' down?

O Mr. Moon,
Just see the clover!
Soon we'll be going
Where the Gray Goose went
When all her money
Was spent, spent, spent!
Down through the clover,
When the revel's over!
Moon, Mr. Moon,
When you comin' down?

O Moon, Mr. Moon,
When you comin' down?
Down where the Good Folk
Dance in a ring,
Down where the Little Folk
Sing?
Moon, Mr. Moon,
When you comin' down?

IN A GARDEN

Thought is a garden wide and old
For airy creatures to explore,
Where grow the great fantastic flowers
With truth for honey at the core.

There like a wild marauding bee
Made desperate by hungry fears,
From gorgeous If to dark Perhaps
I blunder down the dusk of years.

There are sunflowers too in my garden on top of the hill,
Where now in the early September the sun has his will—
The slow autumn sun that goes leisurely, taking his fill
Of life in the orchards and fir-woods so moveless and still;
As if, should they stir, they might break some illusion and spill
The germ of their long summer musing on top of the hill.

The crowds of black spruces in tiers from the valley below,
Ranged round their sky-roofed coliseum, mount row after row.
How often there, rank above rank, they have watched for the slow
Silver-lanterned processions of twilight—the moon's come and go!
How often, as if they expected some bugle to blow,
Announcing a bringer of news they were breathless to know,
They have hushed every leaf,—to hear only the murmurous flow
Of the small mountain river sent up from the valley below!

How still through the sweet summer sun, through the soft summer rain,
They have stood there awaiting the summons should bid them attain
The freedom of knowledge, the last touch of truth to explain
The great golden gist of their brooding, the marvellous train
Of thought they have followed so far, been so strong to sustain,—
The white gospel of sun and the long revelations of rain!

Then the orchards that dot, all in order, the green valley floor,
Every tree with its boughs weighed to earth, like a tent from whose door
Not a lodger looks forth,—yet the signs are there gay and galore,
The great ropes of red fruitage and russet, crisp snow to the core.

Can the dark-eyed Romany here have deserted of yore
Their camp at the coming of frost? Will they seek it no more?
Who dwells in St. Eulalie's village? Who knows the fine lore
Of the tribes of the apple-trees there on the green valley floor?

Who, indeed? From the blue mountain gorge to the dikes by the sea,
Goes that stilly wanderer, small Gaspereau; who but he
Should give the last hint of perfection, the touch that sets free
From the taut string of silence the whisper of beauties to be!
The very sun seems to have tarried, turned back a degree,
To lengthen out noon for the apple folk here by the sea.

What is it? Who comes? What's abroad on the blue mountain side?
A hush has been laid on the leaves and will not be defied.
Is the great Scarlet Hunter at last setting out on his ride
From the North with deliverance now? Were the lights we descried

Last night in the heavens his camp-fire seen far and wide,
The white signal of peace for whose coming the ages have cried?
'Expectancy lingers; fulfilment postponed,' I replied,
When soul said uneasily, 'Who is it haunts your hillside?'

All the while not a word from my sunflowers here on the hill.
And to-night when the stars over Blomidon flower and fill
The blue Northern garden of heaven, so pale and so still,
From the lordly king-aster Aldebaran there by the sill
Of the East, where the moonlight will enter, not one will fulfil
A lordlier lot than my sunflowers here on the hill.

So much for mere fact, mere impression. So much I portray
Of the atmosphere, colour, illusion of one autumn day
In the little Acadian valley above the Grand Pré;
Just the quiet of orchards and firs, where the sun had full sway,
And the river went trolling his soft wander-song to the bay,
While roseberry, aster, and sagaban tangled his way.
Be you their interpreter, reasoner; tell what they say,
These children of silence whose patient regard I portray.

You Londoner, walking in Bishopsgate, strolling the Strand,
Some morning in autumn afford, at a fruit-dealer's stand,
The leisure to look at his apples there ruddy and tanned.
Then ask, when he's smiling to serve you, if choice can command
A Gravenstein grown oversea on Canadian land.
(And just for the whim's sake, for once, you'll have no other brand!)
How teach you to tell them? Pick one, and with that in your hand,
Bethink you a while as you turn again into the Strand.

'What if,' you will say,—so smooth in your hand it will lie,
So round and so firm, of so rich a red to the eye,
Like a dash of Fortuny, a tinge of some Indian dye,
While you turn it and toss, mark the bloom, ere you taste it and try—
'Now what if this grew where the same bright pavilion of sky
Is stretched o'er the valley and hillside he bids me descry,
The windless valley of peace, where the seasons go by,
And the river goes down through the orchards where long shadows lie!'

There's the fruit in your hand, in your ears is the roar of the street,
The pulse of an empire keeping its volume and beat,
Its sure come and go day and night, while we sleep or we eat.
Taste the apple, bite in to the juice—how abundant and sweet!
As sound as your own English heart, and wholesome as wheat,—
There grow no such apples as that in your Bishopsgate Street.

Or perhaps in St. Helen's Place, when your business is done
And the ledgers put by, you will think of the hundred and one

Commissions and errands to do; but what under the sun
Was that, so important? Ah, yes! the new books overrun
The old shelves. It is high time to order a new set begun.
Then off to the joiner's. You enter, to see his plane run
With a long high shriek through the lumber he's working upon.
Then he turns from his shavings to query what you would have done.

But homeward 'tis you who make question. That song of the blade!
And the sharp sweet cry of the wood, what an answer it made!
What stories the joiner must hear, as he plies his clean trade,
Of all the wild life of the forest where long shadows wade
The untrodden moss, and the firs send a journeying shade
So slow through the valley so far from the song of his blade.

Come back to my orchards a moment. They're waiting for you.
How still are the little gray leaves where the pippins peep through!
The boughs where the ribstons hang red are half breaking in two.
Above them September in magical soft Northern blue
Has woven the spell of her silence, like frost or like dew,
Yet warm as a poppy's red dream. When All Saints shall renew
The beauty of summer a while, will their dreaming come true?
Ah, not of my Grand Pré they dream, nor your London and you!

Their life is their own, and the surge of it. All through the spring
They pushed forth their buds, and the rainbirds at twilight would sing.
They put forth their bloom, and the world was as fairy a thing
As a Japanese garden. Then midsummer came with the zing
And the clack of the locust; then fruit time and coolness, to bring
This aftermath deep underfoot with its velvety spring.

And they all the while with the fatherly, motherly care,
Taking sap from the strength of the ground, taking sun from the air,
Taking chance of the frost and the worm, taking courage to dare,
Have given their life that the life might be goodly and fair
In their kind for the seasons to come, with good witness to bear
How the sturdy old race of the apples could give and not spare.
To-morrow the harvest begins. We shall rifle them there
Of the beautiful fruit of their bodies, the crown of their care.

How lovingly then shall the picker set hand to the bough!—
Bid it yield, ere the seed come to earth or the graft to the plough,
Not only sweet life for its kind, as the instincts allow,
That savour and shape may survive generations from now,
But life to its kin who can say, 'I am stronger than thou,'—
Fulfilling a lordlier law than the law of the bough.

I heard before dawn, with planets beginning to quail,—
'Whoso hath life, let him give, that my purpose prevail;

Whoso hath none, let him take, that his strength may be hale.
Behold, I have reckoned the tally, I keep the full tale.
Whoso hath love, let him give, lest his spirit grow stale;
Whoso hath none, let him die; he shall wither and fail.
Behold, I will plenish the loss at the turn of the scale.
He hath law to himself, who hath love; ye shall hope and not quail.'

Then the sun arose, and my sunflowers here on the hill,
Like good little Catholics, turned to the East to fulfil
Their daily observance, receiving his peace and his will,—
The lord of their light who alone bids the darkness be nil,
The lord of their love who alone bids the life in them thrill;
Undismayed and serene, they awaited him here on the hill.

Ah, the patience of earth! Look down at the dark pointed firs;
They are carved out of blackness; one pattern recurs and recurs.
They crowd all the gullies and hillsides, the gashes and spurs,
As silent as death. What an image! How nature avers
The goodness of calm with that taciturn beauty of hers!
As silent as sleep. Yet the life in them climbs and stirs.
They too have received the great law, know that haste but defers
The perfection of time,—the initiate gospeller firs.

So year after year, slow ring upon ring, they have grown,
Putting infinite long-loving care into leafage and cone,
By the old ancient craft of the earth they have pondered and known
In the dead of the hot summer noons, as still as a stone.
Not for them the gay fruit of the thorn, nor the high scarlet roan,
Nor the plots of the deep orchard land where the apples are grown.

In winter the wind, all huddled and shuddering, came
To warm his old bones by the fires of sunset aflame
Behind the black house of the firs. When the moose-birds grew tame
In the lumberers' camps in the woods, what marvellous fame
His talk and the ice of his touch would spread and proclaim,
Of the berg and the floe and the lands without nation or name,
Where the earth and the sky, night and noon, north and south are the same,
The white and awful Nirvana of cold whence he came!

Then April, some twilight picked out with a great yellow star,
Returning, like Hylas long lost and come back with his jar
Of sweet living water at last, having wandered so far,
Leads the heart out of doors, and the eye to the point of a spar,
At whose base in the half-melted snow the first Mayflowers are,—
And there the first robin is pealing below the great star.

So soon, over-soon, the full summer. Within those dark boughs,
Deliberate and far, a faltering reed-note will rouse

The shy transports of earth, till the wood-creatures hear where they house,
And grow bold as the tremble-eared rabbits that nibble and mouse.
While up through the pasture-lot, startling the sheep as they browse,
Where kingbirds and warblers are piercing the heat's golden drowse,
Some girl, whom the sun has made tawny, the wind had to blowse,
Will come there to gentle her lover beneath those dark boughs.

Then out of the hush, when the grasses are frosty and old,
Will the chickadee's tiny alarm against winter be rolled;
And soon, when the ledges and ponds are bitten with cold,
The honk of the geese, that wander-cry stirring and bold,
Will sound through the night, where those hardy mariners hold
The uncharted course through the dark, as it was from of old.

Ah, the life of the woods, how they share and partake of it all,
These evergreens, silent as Indians, solemn and tall!
From the goldenwing's first far-heard awakening call,
The serene flute of the thrush in his high beech hall,
And the pipe of the frog, to the bannered approach of the fall,
And the sullen wind, when snow arrives on a squall,
Trooping in all night from the North with news would appal
Any outposts but these; with a zest they partake of it all.

Lo, out of the hush they seem to mount and aspire!
From basement to tip they have builded, with heed to go higher,
One circlet of branches a year with their lift of green spire.
Nay, rather they seem to repose, having done with desire,
Awaiting the frost, with the fruit scarlet-bright on the brier,
Each purpose fulfilled, each ardour that bade them aspire.

Then hate be afar from the bite of the axe that shall fell
These keepers of solitude, makers of quiet, who dwell
On the Slopes of the North. And clean be the hand that shall quell
The tread of the sap that was wont to go mounting so well,
Round on round with the sun in a spiral, slow cell after cell,
As a bell-ringer climbs in a turret. That resinous smell
From the eighth angel's hand might have risen with the incense to swell
His offering in heaven, when the half-hour's silence befell.

Behold, as the prayers of the saints that went up to God's knees
In John's Revelation, the silence and patience of these
Our brothers of orchard and hill, the unhurrying trees,
To better the burden of earth till the dark suns freeze,
Shall go out to the stars with the sound of Acadian seas,
And the scent of the wood-flowers blowing about their great knees.

To-night when Altair and Alshain are ruling the West,
Whence Boötes is driving his dogs to long hunting addressed;

With Alioth sheer over Blomidon standing at rest;
When Algol is leading the Pleiades over the crest
Of the magical East, and the South puts Alpherat to test
With Menkar just risen; will come, like a sigh from Earth's breast,
The first sob of the tide turning home,—one distraught in his quest
For ever, and calling for ever the wind in the west.

And to-night there will answer the ghost of a sigh on the hill,
So small you would say, Is it wind, or the frost with a will
Walking down through the woods, and to-morrow shall show us his skill
In yellows and reds? So noiseless, it hardly will thrill
The timorous aspens, which tremble when all else is still;
Yet the orchards will know, and the firs be aware on the hill.

'O Night, I am old, I endure. Since my being began,
When out of the dark thy aurora spread up like a fan,
I have founded the lands and the islands; the hills are my plan.
I have covered the pits of the earth with my bridge of one span.
From the Horn to Dunedin unbroken my long rollers ran,
From Pentland and Fastnet and Foyle to Bras d'Or and Manan,
To dredge and upbuild for the creatures of tribe and of clan.
Lo, now who shall end the contriving my fingers began?'

Then the little wind that blows from the great star-drift
Will answer: 'Thou tide in the least of the planets I lift,
Consider the journeys of light. Are thy journeyings swift?
Thy sands are as smoke to the star-banks I huddle and shift.
Peace! I have seeds of the grasses to scatter and sift.
I have freighting to do for the weed and the frail thistle drift.

'O ye apples and firs, great and small are as one in the end.
Because ye had life to the full, and spared not to spend;
Because ye had love of your kind, to cherish and fend;
Held hard the good instinct to thrive, cleaving close to life's trend;

Nor questioned where impulse had origin,—purpose might tend;
Now, beauty is yours, and the freedom whose promptings transcend
Attainment for ever, in death with new being to blend.
O ye orchards and woods, death is naught, love is all in the end.'

Ah, friend of mine over the sea, shall we not discern,
In the life of our brother the beech and our sister the fern,
As St. Francis would call them (his Minorites, too, would we learn!)
In death but a door to new being no creature may spurn,
But must enter for beauty's completion,—pass up in his turn
To the last round of joy, yours and mine, whence to think and discern?

Who shall say 'the last round'? Have I passed by the exit of soul?

From behind the tall door that swings outward, replies no patrol
To our restless Qui vive? when is paid each implacable toll.
Not a fin of the tribes shall return, having cleared the great shoal;
Not a wing of the migrants come back from below the dark knoll;
Yet the zest of the flight and the swimming who fails to extol?
Saith the Riddle, 'The parts are all plain; ye may guess at the whole.'
I guess, 'Immortality, knowledge, survival of Soul.'

To-night, with the orchards below and the firs on the hill
Asleep in the long solemn moonlight and taking no ill,
A hand will open the sluice of the great sea-mill,—
Start the gear and the belts of the tide. Then a murmur will fill
The hollows of midnight with sound, when all else is still,
And stray through the dream of the sunflowers here on the hill.

BAHAMAN

In the crowd that thronged the pierhead, come to see their friends take ship
For new ventures in seafaring, when the hawsers were let slip
And we swung out in the current, with good-byes on every lip,
'Midst the waving caps and kisses, as we dropped down with the tide
And the faces blurred and faded, last of all your hand I spied
Signalling, Farewell, Good fortune! then my heart rose up and cried:
'While the world holds one such comrade, whose sweet durable regard
Would so speed my safe departure, lest home-leaving should be hard,
What care I who keeps the ferry, whether Charon or Cunard!'
Then we cleared the bar, and laid her on the course, the thousand miles
From the Hook to the Bahamas, from midwinter to the isles
Where frost never laid a finger, and eternal summer smiles.
Three days through the surly storm-beat, while the surf-heads threshed and flew,
And the rolling mountains thundered to the trample of the screw,
The black liner heaved and scuffled and strained on, as if she knew.
On the fourth, the round blue morning sparkled there, all light and breeze,
Clean and tenuous as a bubble blown from two immensities,
Shot and coloured with sheer sunlight and the magic of those seas.
In that bright new world of wonder, it was life enough to laze
All day underneath the awnings, and through half-shut eyes to gaze
At the marvel of the sea-blue; and I faltered for a phrase

Should half give you the impression, tell you how the very tint
Justified your finest daring, as if Nature gave the hint,
'Plodders, see Imagination set his pallet without stint!'
Cobalt, gobelin, and azure, turquoise, sapphire, indigo,
Changing from the spectral bluish of a shadow upon snow
To the deep of Canton china,—one unfathomable glow.
And the flying-fish,—to see them in a scurry lift and flee,

Silvery as the foam they sprang from, fragile people of the sea,
Whom their heart's great aspiration for a moment had set free.
From the dim and cloudy ocean, thunder-centred, rosy-verged,
At the lord sun's Sursum Corda, as implicit impulse urged,
Frail as vapour, fine as music, these bright spirit-things emerged;
Like those flocks of small white snowbirds we have seen start up before
Our brisk walk in winter weather by the snowy Scituate shore;
And the tiny shining sea-folk brought you back to me once more.

So we ran down Abaco; and passing that tall sentinel
Black against the sundown, sighted, as the sudden twilight fell,
Nassau light; and the warm darkness breathed on us from breeze and swell.

Stand-by bell and stop of engine; clank of anchor going down;
And we're riding in the roadstead off a twinkling-lighted town,
Low dark shore with boom of breakers and white beach the palm-trees crown.

In the soft wash of the sea air, on the long swing of the tide,
Here for once the dream came true, the voyage ended close beside
The Hesperides in moonlight on mid-ocean where they ride!

And those Hesperidean joy-lands were not strange to you and me.
Just beyond the lost horizon, every time we looked to sea
From Testudo, there they floated, looming plain as plain could be.

Who believed us? 'Myth and fable are a science in our time.'
'Never saw the sea that colour. "Never heard of such a rhyme.'
Well, we've proved it, prince of idlers,—knowledge wrong and faith sublime.
Right were you to follow fancy, give the vaguer instinct room
In a heaven of clear colour, where the spirit might assume
All her elemental beauty, past the fact of sky or bloom.
Paint the vision, not the view,—the touch that bids the sense good-bye,
Lifting spirit at a bound beyond the frontiers of the eye,
To suburb unguessed dominions of the soul's credulity.
Never yet was painter, poet, born content with things that are,—
Must divine from every beauty other beauties greater far,
Till the arc of truth be circled, and her lantern blaze, a star.
This alone is art's ambition, to arrest with form and hue
Dominant ungrasped ideals, known to credence, hid from view,
In a mimic of creation,—to the life, yet fairer too,—
Where the soul may take her pleasure, contemplate perfection's plan,
And returning bring the tidings of his heritage to man,—
News of continents uncharted she has stood tip-toe to scan.
So she fires his gorgeous fancy with a cadence, with a line,
Till the artist wakes within him, and the toiler grows divine,
Shaping the rough world about him nearer to some fair design.
Every heart must have its Indies,—an inheritance unclaimed
In the unsubstantial treasure of a province never named,

Loved and longed for through a lifetime, dull, laborious, and unfamed,

Never wholly disillusioned. Spiritus, read, haeres sit
Patriæ quæ tristia mescit. This alone the great king writ
O'er the tomb of her he cherished in this fair world she must quit.

Love in one farewell for ever, taking counsel to implore
Best of human benedictions on its dead, could ask no more.
The heart's country for a dwelling, this at last is all our lore.
But the fairies at your cradle gave you craft to build a home
In the wide bright world of colour, with the cunning of a gnome;
Blessed you so above your fellows of the tribe that still must roam.
Still across the world they go, tormented by a strange unrest,
And the unabiding spirit knocks for ever at their breast,
Bidding them away to fortune in some undiscovered West;
While at home you sit and call the Orient up at your command,
Master of the iris seas and Prospero of the purple land.
Listen, here was one world-corner matched the cunning of your hand.
Not, my friend, since we were children, and all wonder-tales were true,—
Jason, Hengest, Hiawatha, fairy prince or pirate crew—
Was there ever such a landing in a country strange and new?
Up the harbour where there gathered, fought and revelled many a year,
Swarthy Spaniard, lost Lucayan, Loyalist, and Buccaneer,
'Once upon a time' was now, and 'far across the sea' was here.
Tropic moonlight, in great floods and fathoms pouring through the trees
On a ground as white as sea-froth its fantastic traceries,
While the poincianas, rustling like the rain, moved in the breeze,
Showed a city, coral-streeted, melting in the mellow shine,
Built of creamstone and enchantment, fairy work in every line,
In a velvet atmosphere that bids the heart her haste resign.
Thanks to Julian Hospitator, saint of travellers by sea,
Roving minstrels and all boatmen,—just such vagabonds as we—
On the shaded wharf we landed, rich in leisure, hale and free.

What more would you for God's creatures, but the little tide of sleep?
In a clean white room I wakened, saw the careless sunlight peep
Through the roses at the window, lay and listened to the creep
Of the soft wind in the shutters, heard the palm-tops stirring high,
And that strange mysterious shuffle of the slipshod foot go by.
In a world all glad with colour, gladdest of all things was I;
In a quiet convent garden, tranquil as the day is long,
Here to sit without intrusion of the world or strife or wrong,—
Watch the lizards chase each other, and the green bird make his song;
Warmed and freshened, lulled yet quickened in that Paradisal air,
Motherly and uncapricious, healing every hurt or care,
Wooing body, mind, and spirit, firmly back to strong and fair;
By the Angelus reminded, silence waits the touch of sound,
As the soul waits her awaking to some Gloria profound;

Till the mighty Southern Cross is lighted at the day's last bound.
And if ever your fair fortune make you good Saint Vincent's guest,
At his door take leave of trouble, welcomed to his decent rest,
Of his ordered peace partaker, by his solace healed and blessed;
Where this flowered cloister garden, hidden from the passing view,
Lies behind its yellow walls in prayer the holy hours through:
And beyond, that fairy harbour, floored in malachite and blue.
In that old white-streeted city gladness has her way at last
Under burdens finely poised, and with a freedom unsurpassed,
Move the naked-footed bearers in the blue day deep and vast.
This is Bay Street broad and low-built, basking in its quiet trade;
Here the sponging fleet is anchored; here shell trinkets are displayed;
Here the cable news is posted daily; here the market's made,

With its oranges from Andros, heaps of yam and tamarind,
Red-juiced shadducks from the Current, ripened in the long trade-wind,
Gaudy fish from their sea-gardens, yellow-tailed and azure-tinned.
Here a group of diving boys in bronze and ivory, bright and slim,
Sparkling copper in the high noon, dripping loin-cloth, polished limb,
Poised a moment and then plunged in that deep daylight green and dim.
Here the great rich Spanish laurels spread across the public square
Their dense, solemn shade; and near by, half within the open glare,
Mannerly in their clean cottons, knots of blacks are waiting there
By the court-house, where a magistrate is hearing cases through,
Dealing justice prompt and level, as the sturdy English do,—
One more tent-peg of the Empire, holding that great shelter true.
Last the picture from the town's end, palmed and foam-fringed through the cane,
Where the gorgeous sunset yellows pour aloft and spill and stain
The pure amethystine sea and far faint islands of the main.
Loveliest of the Lucayas, peace be yours till time be done!
In the gray North I shall see you, with your white streets in the sun,
Old pink walls and purple gateways, where the lizards bask and run,
Where the great hibiscus blossoms in their scarlet loll and glow,
And the idling gay bandannas through the hot noons come and go,
While the ever-stirring sea-wind sways the palm-tops to and fro.
Far from stress and storm for ever, dream behind your jalousies,
While the long white lines of breakers crumble on your reefs and keys,
And the crimson oleanders burn against the peacock seas.

THE EAVESDROPPER

In a still room at hush of dawn,
My Love and I lay side by side
And heard the roaming forest wind
Stir in the paling autumn-tide.

I watched her earth-brown eyes grow glad
Because the round day was so fair;
While memories of reluctant night
Lurked in the blue dusk of her hair.

Outside, a yellow maple-tree,
Shifting upon the silvery blue
With small innumerable sound,
Rustled to let the sunlight through.

The livelong day the elvish leaves
Danced with their shadows on the floor;
And the lost children of the wind
Went straying homeward by our door.

And all the swarthy afternoon
We watched the great deliberate sun
Walk through the crimsoned hazy world,
Counting his hilltops one by one.

Then as the purple twilight came
And touched the vines along our eaves,
Another Shadow stood without
And gloomed the dancing of the leaves.

The silence fell on my Love's lips;
Her great brown eyes were veiled and sad
With pondering some maze of dream,
Though all the splendid year was glad.

Restless and vague as a gray wind
Her heart had grown, she knew not why.
But hurrying to the open door,
Against the verge of western sky

I saw retreating on the hills,
Looming and sinister and black,
The stealthy figure swift and huge
Of One who strode and looked not back.

LOW TIDE ON THE GRAND PRÉ

The sun goes down, and over all
These barren reaches by the tide
Such unelusive glories fall,
I almost dream they yet will bide

Until the coming of the tide.

And yet I know that not for us,
By any ecstasy of dream,
He lingers to keep luminous
A little while the grievous stream,
Which frets, uncomforted of dream—

A grievous stream, that to and fro
Athrough the fields of Acadie
Goes wandering, as if to know
Why one beloved face should be
So long from home and Acadie.

Was it a year or lives ago
We took the grasses in our hands,
And caught the summer flying low
Over the waving meadow lands,
And held it there between our hands?

The while the river at our feet—
A drowsy inland meadow stream—
At set of sun the after-heat
Made running gold, and in the gleam
We freed our birch upon the stream.

There down along the elms at dusk
We lifted dripping blade to drift,
Through twilight scented fine like musk,
Where night and gloom awhile uplift,
Nor sunder soul and soul adrift.

And that we took into our hands—
Spirit of life or subtler thing—
Breathed on us there, and loosed the bands
Of death, and taught us, whispering,
The secret of some wonder-thing.

Then all your face grew light, and seemed
To hold the shadow of the sun;
The evening faltered, and I deemed
That time was ripe, and years had done
Their wheeling underneath the sun.

So all desire and all regret,
And fear and memory, were naught;
One to remember or forget
The keen delight our hands had caught;

Morrow and yesterday were naught.

The night has fallen, and the tide . . .
Now and again comes drifting home,
Across these aching barrens wide,
A sigh like driven wind or foam:
In grief the flood is bursting home.

A NORTHERN VIGIL

Here by the gray north sea,
In the wintry heart of the wild,
Comes the old dream of thee,
Guendolen, mistress and child.

The heart of the forest grieves
In the drift against my door;
A voice is under the eaves,
A footfall on the floor.

Threshold, mirror, and hall,
Vacant and strangely aware,
Wait for their soul's recall
With the dumb expectant air.

Here when the smouldering west
Burns down into the sea,
I take no heed of rest
And keep the watch for thee.

I sit by the fire and hear
The restless wind go by,
On the long dirge and drear,
Under the low bleak sky.

When day puts out to sea
And night makes in for land,
There is no lock for thee,
Each door awaits thy hand!

When night goes over the hill
And dawn comes down the dale,
It's O for the wild sweet will
That shall no more prevail!

When the zenith moon is round,

And snow-wraiths gather and run,
And there is set no bound
To love beneath the sun,

O wayward will, come near
The old mad wilful way,
The soft mouth at my ear
With words too sweet to say!

Come, for the night is cold,
The ghostly moonlight fills
Hollow and rift and fold
Of the eerie Ardise hills!

The windows of my room
Are dark with bitter frost,
The stillness aches with doom
Of something loved and lost.

Outside, the great blue star
Burns in the ghostland pale,
Where giant Algebar
Holds on the endless trail.

Come, for the years are long
And silence keeps the door,
Where shapes with the shadows throng
The firelit chamber floor.

Come, for thy kiss was warm,
With the red embers' glare
Across thy folding arm
And dark tumultuous hair!

And though thy coming rouse
The sleep-cry of no bird,
The keepers of the house
Shall tremble at thy word.

Come, for the soul is free!
In all the vast dreamland
There is no lock for thee,
Each door awaits thy hand.

Ah, not in dreams at all,
Fleering, perishing, dim,
But thy old self, supple and tall,
Mistress and child of whim!

The proud imperious guise,
Impetuous and serene,
The sad mysterious eyes,
And dignity of mien!

Yea, wilt thou not return,
When the late hill-winds veer,
And the bright hill-flowers burn
With the reviving year?

When April comes, and the sea
Sparkles as if it smiled,
Will they restore to me
My dark Love, empress and child?

The curtains seem to part;
A sound is on the stair,
As if at the last . . . I start;
Only the wind is there.

Lo, now far on the hills
The crimson fumes uncurled,
Where the caldron mantles and spills
Another dawn on the world!

THE GRAVE-TREE

Let me have a scarlet maple
For the grave-tree at my head,
With the quiet sun behind it,
In the years when I am dead.

Let me have it for a signal,
Where the long winds stream and stream,
Clear across the dim blue distance,
Like at horn blown in at dream;

Scarlet when the April vanguard
Bugles up the laggard Spring,
Scarlet when the bannered Autumn
Marches by unwavering.

It will comfort me with honey
When the shining rifts and showers
Sweep across the purple valley

And bring back the forest flowers.

It will be my leafy cabin,
Large enough when June returns
And I hear the golden thrushes
Flute and hesitate by turns.

And in fall, some yellow morning,
When the stealthy frost has come,
Leaf by leaf it will befriend me
As with comrades going home.

Let me have the Silent Valley
And the hill that fronts the east,
So that I can watch the morning
Redden and the stars released.

Leave me in the Great Lone Country,
For I shall not be afraid
With the shy moose and the beaver
There within my scarlet shade.

I would sleep, but not too soundly,
Where the sunning partridge drums,
Till the crickets hush before him
When the Scarlet Hunter comes.

That will be in warm September,
In the stillness of the year,
When the river-blue is deepest
And the other world is near.

When the apples burn their reddest
And the corn is in the sheaves,
I shall stir and waken lightly
At a footfall in the leaves.

It will be the Scarlet Hunter
Come to tell me time is done;
On the idle hills for ever
There will stand the idle sun.

There the wind will stay to whisper
Many wonders to the reeds;
But I shall not fear to follow
Where my Scarlet Hunter leads.

I shall know him in the darkling

Murmur of the river bars,
While his feet are on the mountains
Treading out the smouldering stars.

I shall know him, in the sunshine
Sleeping in my scarlet tree,
Long before he halts beside it
Stooping down to summon me.

Then fear not, my friends, to leave me
In the boding autumn vast;
There are many things to think of
When the roving days are past.

Leave me by the scarlet maple,
When the journeying shadows fail,
Waiting till the Scarlet Hunter
Pass upon the endless trail.

A SEAMARK

Cold, the dull cold! What ails the sun,
And takes the heart out of the day?
What makes the morning look so mean,
The Common so forlorn and gray?

The wintry city's granite heart
Beats on in iron mockery,
And like the roaming mountain rains,
I hear the thresh of feet go by.

It is the lonely human surf
Surging through alleys chill with grime,
The muttering churning ceaseless floe
Adrift out of the North of time.

Fades, it all fades! I only see
The poster with its reds and blues
Bidding the heart stand still to take
Its desolating stab of news.

That intimate and magic name:
'Dead in Samoa.' . . . Cry your cries,
O city of the golden dome,
Under the gray Atlantic skies!

But I have wander-biddings now.
Far down the latitudes of sun,
An island mountain of the sea,
Piercing the green and rosy zone,

Goes up into the wondrous day.
And there the brown-limbed island men
Are bearing up for burial,
Within the sun's departing ken,

The master of the roving kind.
And there where time will set no mark
For his irrevocable rest,
Under the spacious melting dark,

With all the nomad tented stars
About him, they have laid him down
Above the crumbling of the sea,
Beyond the turmoil of renown.

O all you hearts about the world
In whom the truant gipsy blood,
Under the frost of this pale time,
Sleeps like the daring sap and flood

That dream of April and reprieve!
You whom the haunted vision drives,
Incredulous of home and ease,
Perfection's lovers all your lives!

You whom the wander-spirit loves
To lead by some forgotten clue
For ever vanishing beyond
Horizon brinks for ever new;

The road, unmarked, ordained, whereby
Your brothers of the field and air
Before you, faithful, blind, and glad,
Emerged from chaos pair by pair;

The road whereby you too must come,
In the unvexed and fabled years
Into the country of your dream,
With all your knowledge in arrears!

You who can never quite forget
Your glimpse of Beauty as she passed,
The well-head where her knee was pressed,

The dew wherein her foot was cast;

O you who bid the paint and clay
Be glorious when you are dead,
And fit the plangent words in rhyme
Where the dark secret lurks unsaid;

You brethren of the light-heart guild,
The mystic fellowcraft of joy,
Who tarry for the news of truth,
And listen for some vast ahoy

Blown in from sea, who crowd the wharves
With eager eyes that wait the ship
Whose foreign tongue may fill the world
With wondrous tales from lip to lip;

Our restless loved adventurer,
On secret orders come to him,
Has slipped his cable, cleared the reef,
And melted on the white sea-rim.

O granite hills, go down in blue!
And like green clouds in opal calms,
You anchored islands of the main,
Float up your loom of feathery palms!

For deep within your dales, where lies
A valiant earthling stark and dumb,
This savage undiscerning heart
Is with the silent chiefs who come

To mourn their kin and bear him gifts,—
Who kiss his hand, and take their place,
This last night he receives his friends,
The journey-wonder on his face.

He 'was not born for age.' Ah no,
For everlasting youth is his!
Part of the lyric of the earth
With spring and leaf and blade he is.

'Twill nevermore be April now
But there will lurk a thought of him
At the street corners, gay with flowers
From rainy valleys purple-dim.

O chiefs, you do not mourn alone!

In that stern North where mystery broods,
Our mother grief has many sons
Bred in those iron solitudes.

It does not help them, to have laid
Their coil of lightning under seas;
They are as impotent as you
To mend the loosened wrists and knees.

And yet how many a harvest night,
When the great luminous meteors flare
Along the trenches of the dusk,
The men who dwell beneath the Bear,

Seeing those vagrants of the sky
Float through the deep beyond their hark,
Like Arabs through the wastes of air,—
A flash, a dream, from dark to dark,—

Must feel the solemn large surmise:
By a dim, vast and perilous way
We sweep through undetermined time,
Illumining this quench of clay,

A moment staunched, then forth again.
Ah, not alone you climb the steep
To set your loving burden down
Against the mighty knees of sleep.

With you we hold the sombre faith
Where creeds are sown like rain at sea;
And leave the loveliest child of earth
To slumber where he longed to be.

His fathers lit the dangerous coast
To steer the daring merchant home;
His courage lights the darkling port
Where every sea-worn sail must come.

And since he was the type of all
That strain in us which still must fare,
The fleeting migrant of a day,
Heart-high, outbound for otherwhere,

Now therefore, where the passing ships
Hang on the edges of the noon,
And Northern liners trail their smoke
Across the rising yellow moon,

Bound for his home, with shuddering screw
That beats its strength out into speed,
Until the pacing watch descries
On the sea-line a scarlet seed

Smoulder and kindle and set fire
To the dark selvedge of the night,
The deep blue tapestry of stars,
Then sheet the dome in pearly light,

There in perpetual tides of day,
Where men may praise him and deplore,
The place of his lone grave shall be
A seamark set for evermore,

High on a peak adrift with mist,
And round whose bases, far beneath
The snow-white wheeling tropic birds,
The emerald dragon breaks his teeth.

AT COLUMBINE'S GRAVE

Ah, Pierrot,
Where is thy Columbine?
What vandal could untwine
That gay rose-rope of thine,
And spill thy joy like wine,
Poor Pierrot?

Ah, Pierrot,
The moon is rising red
Above thy grief-bowed head;
Thy roses are all shed.
And Columbine is dead!
Poor Pierrot!

Ah, Pierrot,
Kneel down beside her tomb.
The gray wind of the gloom,
In the world's empty room,
Has shut the door of doom.
Poor Pierrot!

Ah, Pierrot,
Is there not one sweet word

Of brook or breeze or bird
A mortal ever heard,
Could cheer thee—not one word,
Poor Pierrot?

Ah, Pierrot,
A thousand times the spring
Will come to dance and sing
Up the green earth, and bring
Joy to each living thing,
Poor Pierrot!

But, Pierrot,
When all that pomp shall pass
Her lowly house in the grass,
Will any say, 'Alas,
Poor Columbine; alas,
Poor Pierrot'?

Ah, Pierrot,
Thy loving tears in vain
Shall fall like quiet rain
For her; till the stars wane,
She will not come again,
Poor Pierrot.

Yet, Pierrot,
The mighty Mother now
Hath her in care somehow.
Listen, and clear that brow:
'O earthling, grieve not thou,
Poor Pierrot!

'Ah, Pierrot,
Here on my cool green floor
I do transmute, restore,
All things once fair before
To beauty more and more.
Poor Pierrot!'

THE LAST ROOM

There, close the door!
I shall not need these lodgings any more.
Now that I go, dismantled wall and floor
Reproach me and deplore.

'How well,' they say,
'And silently we served you day by day,—
Took every mood, as you were sad or gay
In that strange mortal way.'

These patient walls
Seem half to know what suffering befalls
The steadfast soul whom destiny appalls
And circumstance enthralls.

A solitude,
Dim as an orchard, quiet as a wood;
My six mute friends who stolidly withstood
Tempest and turmoil rude;

One door, wherethrough
Came human love in little gown and shoe;
One window, where great Nature robed in blue
Smiled benediction too;

And one hearthstone,
The kind primeval fire-god made his own,—
Bringing us back the wood life we had known,
With lighted log and cone.

Here life was spent
To glorify one mortal tenement,
Where freedom turned the key on discontent
And bade the world relent.

Great friendship here
Turned falsehood out of doors without a fear,
And brought the golden age of dreamers near
For one all too brief year.

Good friends, good-bye!
The soul is but a child; hear its poor cry,
'Remember in what lovers' tenancy
We lived here, she and I!'

Will you forget
Spilt fragrances of rose and cigarette,
And those faint odours more delirious yet,
Marked in Time's margin, Stet?

Will you not hold
Some echo of bright laughter uncontrolled,

As water bubbling out of jugs of gold,
Until the world is old?

With one farewell
I leave you now, with not a word to tell
Where comedy and moonshine used to dwell
Within a brick-built cell.

In days to be
Others shall laugh here, roister and make free,
Be bold or gay,—but no such comedy
As blessed this life for me.

In nights to come
Others shall dream here, radiant or glum,
Pondering the book God gives us each to thumb,—
Our page to solve and sum,—

But nevermore
Such moonshine as would tread this square of floor,
And for love's sake illumine and explore
The dark at sorrow's core.

'The sad Pierrot
Lived here and loved,'—how will the story go?—
'Caught rapture from the moment's zest or woe,
One winter long ago.

'Here did Pierrette
Throw dice with destiny to pay love's debt,
Gay, kind, and fearless, without one regret
When the last stake was set.'

Peace, peace, fair room,—
My peace be with them still, through shine and gloom,
Who here may sojourn, ere they too resume
This search for house and home.

Now, to explore!
The impatient wind is in the corridor;
Fate lays a finger on my sleeve once more;
And I must close this door.

THE UNRETURNING

The old eternal spring once more

Comes back the sad eternal way,
With tender rosy light before
The going-out of day.

The great white moon across my door
A shadow in the twilight stirs;
But now for ever comes no more
That wondrous look of Hers.

Bliss Carman - An Appreciation

How many Canadians—how many even among the few who seek to keep themselves informed of the best in contemporary literature, who are ever on the alert for the new voices—realise, or even suspect, that this Northern land of theirs has produced a poet of whom it may be affirmed with confidence and assurance that he is of the great succession of English poets? Yet such—strange and unbelievable though it may seem—is in very truth the case, that poet being (to give him his full name) William Bliss Carman. Canada has full right to be proud of her poets, a small body though they are; but not only does Mr. Carman stand high and clear above them all—his place (and time cannot but confirm and justify the assertion) is among those men whose poetry is the shining glory of that great English literature which is our common heritage.

If any should ask why, if what has been just said is so, there has been—as must be admitted—no general recognition of the fact in the poet's home land, I would answer that there are various and plausible, if not good, reasons for it.

First of all, the poet, as thousands more of our young men of ambition and confidence have done, went early to the United States, and until recently, except for rare and brief visits to his old home down by the sea, has never returned to Canada—though for all that, I am able to state, on his own authority, he is still a Canadian citizen. Then all his books have had their original publication in the United States, and while a few of them have subsequently carried the imprints of Canadian publishers, none of these can be said ever to have made any special effort to push their sale. Another reason for the fact above mentioned is that Mr. Carman has always scorned to advertise himself, while his work has never been the subject of the log-rolling and booming which the work of many another poet has had—to his ultimate loss. A further reason is that he follows a rule of his own in preparing his books for publication. Most poets publish a volume of their work as soon as, through their industry and perseverance, they have material enough on hand to make publication desirable in their eyes. Not so with Mr. Carman, however, his rule being not to publish until he has done sufficient work of a certain general character or key to make a volume. As a result, you cannot fully know or estimate his work by one book, or two books, or even half a dozen; you must possess or be familiar with every one of the score and more volumes which contain his output of poetry before you can realise how great and how many-sided is his genius.

It is a common remark on the part of those who respond readily to the vigorous work of Kipling, or Masefield, even our own Service, that Bliss Carman's poetry has no relation to or concern with ordinary, everyday life. One would suppose that most persons who cared for poetry at all turned to it as a relief from or counter to the burdens and vexations of the daily round; but in any event, the remark referred to seems to me to indicate either the most casual acquaintance with Mr. Carman's work, or a complete misunderstanding and misapprehension of the meaning of it. I grant that you will find little or nothing in it all to remind you of the grim realities and vexing social problems of this modern existence of ours; but to say or to suggest that these things do not exist for Mr. Carman is to say or to suggest something which is the reverse of true. The truth is, he is aware of them as only one with the sensitive organism of a poet can be; but he does not feel that he has a call or mission to remedy them, and still less to sing of them. He therefore leaves the immediate problems of the day to those who choose, or are led, to occupy themselves therewith, and turns resolutely away to dwell upon those things which for him possess infinitely greater importance.

"What are they?" one who knows Mr. Carman only as, say, a lyrist of spring or as a singer of the delights of vagabondia probably will ask in some wonder. Well, the things which concern him above all, I would answer, are first, and naturally, the beauty and wonder of this world of ours, and next the mystery of the earthly pilgrimage of the human soul out of eternity and back into it again.

The poems in the present volume—which, by the way, can boast the high honor of being the very first regular Canadian edition of his work—will be evidence ample and conclusive to every reader, I am sure, of the place which

The perennial enchanted
Lovely world and all its lore

occupy in the heart and soul of Bliss Carman, as well as of the magical power with which he is able to convey the deep and unfailing satisfaction and delight which they possess for him. They, however, represent his latest period (he has had three well-defined periods), comprising selections from three of his last published volumes: The Rough Rider, Echoes from Vagabondia, and April Airs, together with a number of new poems, and do not show, except here and there and by hints and flashes, how great is his preoccupation with the problem of man's existence—

—the hidden import
Of man's eternal plight.

This is manifest most in certain of his earlier books, for in these he turns and returns to the greatest of all the problems of man almost constantly, probing, with consummate and almost unrivalled use of the art of expression, for the secret which surely, he clearly feels, lies hidden somewhere, to be discovered if one could but pierce deeply enough. Pick up Behind the Arras, and as you turn over page after page you cannot but observe how incessantly the poet's mind—like the minds of his two great masters, Browning and Whitman—works at this problem. In "Behind the Arras," the title poem; "In the Wings," "The Crimson House," "The Lodger," "Beyond the Gamut," "The Juggler"—yes, in every poem in the book—he takes up and handles the strange thing we know as, or call, life, turning it now this way, now that, in an effort to find out its meaning and purpose. He comes but little nearer success in this than do most of the rest of men, of course; but the magical and ever-fresh beauty of his expression, the haunting melody of his lines, the variety of his images and figures and the depth and range of his thought, put his searchings and ponderings in a class by themselves.

Lengthy quotation from Mr. Carman's books is not permitted here, and I must guide myself accordingly, though with reluctance, because I believe that in a study such as this the subject should be allowed to speak for himself as much as possible. In "Behind the Arras" the poet describes the passage from life to death as

A cadence dying down unto its source
In music's course,

and goes on to speak of death as

—the broken rhythm of thought and man,
The sweep and span
Of memory and hope
About the orbit where they still must grope
For wider scope,

To be through thousand springs restored, renewed,
With love imbrued,
With increments of will
Made strong, perceiving unattainment still
From each new skill.

Now follow some verses from "Behind the Gamut," to my mind the poet's greatest single achievement;

As fine sand spread on a disc of silver,
At some chord which bids the motes combine,
Heeding the hidden and reverberant impulse,
Shifts and dances into curve and line,

The round earth, too, haply, like a dust-mote,
Was set whirling her assigned sure way,
Round this little orb of her ecliptic
To some harmony she must obey.

And what of man?

Linked to all his half-accomplished fellows,
Through unfrontiered provinces to range—
Man is but the morning dream of nature,
Roused to some wild cadence weird and strange.

Here, now, are some verses from "Pulvis et Umbra," which is to be found in Mr. Carman's first book, Low
Tide on Grand Pré, and in which the poet addresses a moth which a storm has blown into his window:

For man walks the world with mourning
Down to death and leaves no trace,
With the dust upon his forehead,
And the shadow on his face.

Pillared dust and fleeing shadow
As the roadside wind goes by,
And the fourscore years that vanish

In the twinkling of an eye.

"Pillared dust and fleeing shadow." Where in all our English literature will one find the life history of man summed up more briefly and, at the same time, more beautifully, than in that wonderful line? Now follows a companion verse to those just quoted, taken from "Lord of My Heart's Elation," which stands in the forefront of From the Green Book of the Bards. It may be remarked here that while the poet recurs again and again to some favorite thought or idea, it is never in the same words. His expression is always new and fresh, showing how deep and true is his inspiration. Again it is man who is pictured:

A fleet and shadowy column
Of dust and mountain rain,
To walk the earth a moment
And be dissolved again.

But while Mr. Carman's speculations upon life's meaning and the mystery of the future cannot but appeal to the thoughtful-minded, it is as an interpreter of nature that he makes his widest appeal. Bliss Carman, I must say here, and emphatically, is no mere landscape-painter; he never, or scarcely ever, paints a picture of nature for its own sake. He goes beyond the outward aspect of things and interprets or translates for us with less keen senses as only a poet whose feeling for nature is of the deepest and profoundest, who has gone to her whole-heartedly and been taken close to her warm bosom, can do. Is this not evident from these verses from "The Great Return"—originally called "The Pagan's Prayer," and for some inscrutable reason to be found only in the limited Collected Poems, issued in two stately volumes in 1905.

When I have lifted up my heart to thee,
Thou hast ever hearkened and drawn near,
And bowed thy shining face close over me,
Till I could hear thee as the hill-flowers hear.

When I have cried to thee in lonely need,
Being but a child of thine bereft and wrung,
Then all the rivers in the hills gave heed;
And the great hill-winds in thy holy tongue—

That ancient incommunicable speech—
The April stars and autumn sunsets know—
Soothed me and calmed with solace beyond reach
Of human ken, mysterious and low.

Who can read or listen to those moving lines without feeling that Mr. Carman is in very truth a poet of nature—nay, Nature's own poet? But how could he be other when, in "The Breath of the Reed" (From the Green Book of the Bards), he makes the appeal?

Make me thy priest, O Mother,
And prophet of thy mood,
With all the forest wonder
Enraptured and imbued.

As becomes such a poet, and particularly a poet whose birth-month is April, Mr. Carman sings much of the early spring. Again and again he takes up his woodland pipe, and lo! Pan himself and all his train troop joyously before us. Yet the singer's notes for all his singing never become wearied or strident; his airs are ever new and fresh; his latest songs are no less spontaneous and winning than were his first, written how many years ago, while at the same time they have gained in beauty and melody. What heart will not stir to the vibrant music of his immortal "Spring Song," which was originally published in the first Songs from Vagabondia, and the opening verses of which follow?

Make me over, mother April,
When the sap begins to stir!
When thy flowery hand delivers
All the mountain-prisoned rivers,
And thy great heart beats and quivers
To revive the days that were,
Make me over, mother April,
When the sap begins to stir!

Take my dust and all my dreaming,
Count my heart-beats one by one,
Send them where the winters perish;
Then some golden noon recherish
And restore them in the sun,
Flower and scent and dust and dreaming,
With their heart-beats every one!

That poem is sufficient in itself to prove that Bliss Carman has full right and title to be called Spring's own lyrist, though it may be remarked here that not all his spring poems are so unfeignedly joyous. Many of them indeed, have a touch, or more than a touch, of wistfulness, for the poet knows well that sorrow lurks under all joy, deep and well hidden though it may be.

Mr. Carman sings equally finely, though perhaps not so frequently, of summer and the other seasons; but as he has other claims upon our attention, I shall forbear to labor the fact, particularly as the following collection demonstrates it sufficiently. One of those other claims is as a writer of sea poetry. Few poets, it may be said, have pictured the majesty and the mystery, the beauty and the terror of the sea, better than he. His Ballads of Lost Haven is a veritable treasure-house for those whose spirits find kinship in wide expanses of moving waters. One of the best known poems in this volume is "The Gravedigger," which opens thus:

Oh, the shambling sea is a sexton old,
And well his work is done.
With an equal grave for lord and knave,
He buries them every one.

Then hoy and rip, with a rolling hip,
He makes for the nearest shore;
And God, who sent him a thousand ship,
Will send him a thousand more;
But some he'll save for a bleaching grave,

And shoulder them in to shore—
Shoulder them in, shoulder them in,
Shoulder them in to shore.

In "The City of the Sea" (Last Songs from Vagabondia) Mr. Carman speaks of the seabells sounding

The eternal cadence of sea sorrow
For Man's lot and immemorial wrong—
The lost strains that haunt the human dwelling
With the ghost of song.

Elsewhere he speaks of

The great sea, mystic and musical.

And here from another poem is a striking picture:

... the old sea
Seems to whimper and deplore
Mourning like a childless crone
With her sorrow left alone—
The eternal human cry
To the heedless passer-by.

I have said above that Mr. Carman has had three distinct periods, and intimated that the poems in the following collection are of his third period. The first period may be said to be represented by the Low Tide and Behind the Arras volumes, while the second is displayed in the three volumes of Songs from Vagabondia, which he published in association with his friend Richard Hovey. Bliss Carman was from the first too original and individual a poet to be directly influenced by anyone else; but there can be no doubt that his friendship with Hovey helped to turn him from over-preoccupation with mysteries which, for all their greatness, are not for man to solve, to an intenser realisation of the beauty and loveliness of the world about him and of the joys of human fellowship. The result is seen in such poems as "Spring Song," quoted in part above, and his perhaps equally well-known "The Joys of the Road," which appeared in the same volume with that poem, and a few verses from which follow:

Now the joys of the road are chiefly these:
A crimson touch on the hardwood trees;

A vagrant's morning wide and blue,
In early fall, when the wind walks, too;

A shadowy highway cool and brown,
Alluring up and enticing down

From rippled waters and dappled swamp,
From purple glory to scarlet pomp;

The outward eye, the quiet will,

And the striding heart from hill to hill.

Some of the finest of arman's work is contained in his elegiac or memorial poems, in which he commemorates Keats, Shelley, William Blake, Lincoln, Stevenson, and other men for whom he has a kindred feeling, and also friends whom he has loved and lost. Listen to these moving lines from "Non Omnis Moriar," written in memory of Gleeson White, and to be found in Last Songs from Vagabondia:

There is a part of me that knows,
Beneath incertitude and fear,
I shall not perish when I pass
Beyond mortality's frontier;

But greatly having joyed and grieved,
Greatly content, shall hear the sigh
Of the strange wind across the lone
Bright lands of taciturnity.

In patience therefore I await
My friend's unchanged benign regard,—
Some April when I too shall be
Spilt water from a broken shard.

In "The White Gull," written for the centenary of the birth of Shelley in 1892, and included in By the Aurelian Wall, he thus apostrophizes that clear and shining spirit:

O captain of the rebel host,
Lead forth and far!
Thy toiling troopers of the night
Press on the unavailing fight;
The sombre field is not yet lost,
With thee for star.

Thy lips have set the hail and haste
Of clarions free
To bugle down the wintry verge
Of time forever, where the surge
Thunders and trembles on a waste
And open sea.

In "A Seamark," a threnody for Robert Louis Stevenson, which appears in the same volume, the poet hails "R.L.S." (of whose tribe he may be said to be truly one) as

The master of the roving kind,

and goes on:

O all you hearts about the world
In whom the truant gypsy blood,

Under the frost of this pale time,
Sleeps like the daring sap and flood
That dreams of April and reprieve!
You whom the haunted vision drives,
Incredulous of home and ease.
Perfection's lovers all your lives!

You whom the wander-spirit loves
To lead by some forgotten clue
Forever vanishing beyond
Horizon brinks forever new;
Our restless loved adventurer,
On secret orders come to him,
Has slipped his cable, cleared the reef,
And melted on the white sea-rim.

"Perfection's lovers all your lives." Of these, it may be said without qualification, is Bliss Carman himself.

No summary of Mr. Carman's work, however cursory, would be worthy of the name if it omitted mention of his ventures in the realm of Greek myth. From the Book of Myths is made up of work of that sort, every poem in it being full of the beauty of phrase and melody of which Mr. Carman alone has the secret. The finest poems in the book, barring the opening one, "Overlord," are "Daphne," "The Dead Faun," "Hylas," and "At Phædra's Tomb," but I can do no more here than name them, for extracts would fail to reveal their full beauty. And beauty, after all is said, is the first and last thing with Mr. Carman. As he says himself somewhere:

The joy of the hand that hews for beauty
Is the dearest solace under the sun.

And again

The eternal slaves of beauty
Are the masters of the world.

A slave—a happy, willing slave—to beauty is the poet himself, and the world can never repay him for the message of beauty which he has brought it.

Kindred to From the Book of Myths, but much more important, is Sappho: One Hundred Lyrics, one of the most successful of the numerous attempts which have been made to recapture the poems by that high priestess of song which remain to us only in fragments. Mr. Carman, as Charles G. D. Roberts points out in an introduction to the volume, has made no attempt here at translation or paraphrasing; his venture has been "the most perilous and most alluring in the whole field of poetry"—that of imaginative and, at the same time, interpretive construction. Brief quotation again would fail to convey an adequate idea of the exquisiteness of the work, and all I can do, therefore, is to urge all lovers of real poetry to possess themselves of Sappho: One Hundred Lyrics, for it is literally a storehouse of lyric beauty.

I must not fail here to speak of From the Book of Valentines, which contains some lovely things, notably "At the Great Release." This is not only one of the finest of all Mr. Carman's poems, but it is also one of the finest poems of our time. It is a love poem, and no one possessing any real feeling for poetry can read it without experiencing that strange thrill of the spirit which only the highest form of poetry can communicate. "Morning and Evening," "In an Iris Meadow," and "A letter from Lesbos" must be also mentioned. In the last named poem, Sappho is represented as writing to Gorgo, and expresses herself in these moving words:

If the high gods in that triumphant time
Have calendared no day for thee to come
Light-hearted to this doorway as of old,
Unmoved I shall behold their pomps go by—
The painted seasons in their pageantry,
The silvery progressions of the moon,
And all their infinite ardors unsubdued,
Pass with the wind replenishing the earth

Incredulous forever I must live
And, once thy lover, without joy behold,
The gradual uncounted years go by,
Sharing the bitterness of all things made.

Mention must be now made of Songs of the Sea Children, which can be described only as a collection of the sweetest and tenderest love lyrics written in our time—

—the lyric songs
The earthborn children sing,
When wild-wood laughter throngs
The shy bird-throats of spring;
When there's not a joy of the heart
But flies like a flag unfurled,
And the swelling buds bring back
The April of the world.

So perfect and complete are these lyrics that it would be almost sacrilege to quote any of them unless entire. Listen however, to these verses:

The day is lost without thee,
The night has not a star.
Thy going is an empty room
Whose door is left ajar.

Depart: it is the footfall
Of twilight on the hills.
Return: and every rood of ground
Breaks into daffodils.

There are those who will have it that Bliss Carman has been away from Canada so long that he has ceased to be, in a real sense, a Canadian. Such assume rather than know, for a very little study of his work would show them that it is shot through and through with the poet's feeling for the land of his birth. Memories of his childhood and youthful years down by the sea are still fresh in Mr. Carman's mind, and inspire him again and again in his writing. "A Remembrance," at the beginning of the present collection, may be pointed to as a striking instance of this, but proof positive is the volume, Songs from a Northern Garden, for it could have been written only by a Canadian, born and bred, one whose heart and soul thrill to the thought of Canada. I would single out from this volume for special mention as being "Canadian" in the fullest sense "In a Grand Pré Garden," "The Keeper's Silence," "At Home and Abroad," "Killoleet," and "Above the Gaspereau," but have no space to quote from them.

But Mr. Carman is not only a Canadian, he is also a Briton; and evidence of this is his Ode on the Coronation, written on the occasion of the crowning of King Edward VII in 1902. This poem—the very existence of which is hardly known among us—ought to be put in the hands of every child and youth who speaks the English tongue, for no other, I dare maintain—nothing by Kipling, or Newbolt, or any other of our so-called "Imperial singers"—expresses more truly and more movingly the deep feeling of love and reverence which the very thought of England evokes in every son of hers, even though it may never have been his to see her white cliffs rise or to tread her storied ground:

O England, little mother by the sleepless Northern tide,
Having bred so many nations to devotion, trust, and pride,
Very tenderly we turn
With welling hearts that yearn
Still to love you and defend you,—let the sons of men discern
Wherein your right and title, might and majesty, reside.

In concluding this, I greatly fear, lamentably inadequate study, I come to the collection which follows, and which, as intimated above, represents the work of Mr. Carman's latest period. I must say at once that, while I yield to no one in admiration for Low Tide and the other books of that period, or for the work of the second period, as represented by the Songs from Vagabondia volumes, I have no hesitation in declaring that I regard the poet's work of the past few years with even higher admiration. It may not possess the force and vigor of the work which preceded it; but anything seemingly missing in that respect is more than made up for me by increased beauty and clarity of expression. The mysticism—verging, or more than verging, at times on symbolism—which marked his earlier poems, and which hung, as it were, as a veil between them and the reader, has gone, and the poet's thought or theme now lies clearly before us as in a mirror. What—to take a verse from the following pages at random—could be more pellucid, more crystal clear in expression—what indeed, could come closer to that achieving of the impossible at which every real poet must aim—than this from "In Gold Lacquer".

Gold are the great trees overhead,
And gold the leaf-strewn grass,
As though a cloth of gold were spread
To let a seraph pass.
And where the pageant should go by,
Meadow and wood and stream,
The world is all of lacquered gold,
Expectant as a dream.

The poet, happily, has fully recovered from the serious illness which laid him low some two years ago, and which for a time caused his friends and admirers the gravest concern, and so we may look forward hopefully to seeing further volumes of verse come from the press to make certain his name and fame. But if, for any reason, this should not be—which the gods forfend!—Later Poems, I dare affirm, must and will be regarded as the fine flower and crowning achievement of the genius and art of Bliss Carman.

R. H. HATHAWAY.
Toronto, 1921.

Bliss Carman – A Short Biography

William Bliss Carman was born in Fredericton, in New Brunswick on April 15th 1861. 'Bliss' was his mother's maiden name. She was descended from Daniel Bliss of Concord, Massachusetts, who was the great-grandfather to Ralph Waldo Emerson.

Carman was educated at Fredericton Collegiate School. Here, under the influence of the headmaster George Robert Parkin, he gained an appreciation of classical literature and was introduced to the poetry of many of the Pre-Raphaelites especially Dante Gabriel Rossetti and Algernon Charles Swinburne.

From here he graduated to the University of New Brunswick, obtaining his B.A. there in 1881. As is common with so many writers his first published piece was for the University magazine and for Carman that was in 1879.

England now beckoned and he spent a year at Oxford and then the University of Edinburgh (1882–1883). He returned home to Canada to work on his M.A. which he obtained from the University of New Brunswick in 1884.

Tragically his father died in January, 1885, followed by his mother in February of the following year. Carman now enrolled in Harvard University for a year. There he met and was part of a literary circle that included the American poet Richard Hovey, who would become his close friend, and later collaborator, on the successful Vagabondia poetry series. Carman and Hovey were members of the "Visionists" circle along with Herbert Copeland and F. Holland Day, who would later form the Boston publishing firm Copeland & Day and, in turn, launch Vagabondia.

After Harvard Carman briefly returned to Canada, but was back in Boston by February of 1890 saying "Boston is one of the few places where my critical education and tastes could be of any use to me in earning money. New York and London are about the only other places." However, he was unable to find work in Boston but was more successful in New York becoming the literary editor of the semi-religious New York Independent. There he helped Canadian poets get published and introduced them to a wider readership than they could receive in Canada.

However, Carman and work as an editor were not destined for a long career together and he was dismissed in 1892. There followed short stays with Current Literature, Cosmopolitan, The Chap-Book, and The Atlantic Monthly. Whilst these appointments provided the basis for a career and an income he was not suited to their demands. From 1895 he would only work as a contributor to magazines and newspapers whilst he worked on his volumes of poetry.

Carman first published a book of poetry in 1893 with Low Tide on Grand Pré. He had written the title poem in the summer of 1886 and it had (whilst he was still at Harvard) been published in the spring of 1887 by Atlantic Monthly. Despite its critical acceptance there was no Canadian company prepared to publish the volume. When an American company did so it went bankrupt. Life was becoming difficult for the young poet.

The following year was decidedly better. His partnership with Richard Hovey had given birth to Songs of Vagabondia and it was published by their friends at Copeland & Day. It was an immediate success. The young men were delighted at such a reception. It quickly sold out and was re-printed a number of times. Although these re-prints were small (usually 500-1000 copies) they were frequent.

On the back of this success they would write a further three volumes, which in their turn were almost as successful. They quickly became the center of a cult following, especially among students who empathized with the poetry's anti-materialistic themes, its celebration of personal freedom, and its glorification of comradeship."

The success of Songs of Vagabondia prompted the Boston firm, Stone & Kimball, to reissue Low Tide on Grand Pré and to hire Carman as the editor of its literary journal, The Chapbook. This ceased after a year when the company relocated and Carman expressed his desire to remain in Boston.

In 1885 Carman brought out Behind the Arras, a somewhat more serious and philosophical work centered on the premise of a long meditation using the speaker's house and its many rooms as a symbol of life and the choices to be made. However, the idea and its execution did not quite meld.

Signficantly, in 1896, Carman met Mrs Mary Perry King, who rapidly became patron, adviser and sometime lover. She put money in his pocket, and food in his mouth and, when he struck bottom, often repaired his confidence as well as helping to sell the work. She also later became his writing collaborator on two verse dramas.

Mitchell Kennerley, Carman's roommate wrote that, "On the rare occasions they had intimate relations they always advised me of by leaving a bunch of violets — Mary favorite flower — on the pillow of my bed." If her husband, Dr. King, knew of this arrangement he seems not to have objected. He was a great supporter of Carman's career and seemingly his wife's complicated involvement with that.

In 1897 Carman published Ballad of Lost Haven, a collection of poetry about the sea. Its notable poems include the macabre sea shanty, The Gravedigger. The following year, 1898, came By the Aurelian Wall, the title poem itself was an elegy to John Keats and the book a collection of formal elegies.

In 1899 his publisher, Lamson, Wolffe was taken over by the Boston firm of Small, Maynard & Co., who had also acquired the rights to Low Tide on Grand Pré. The copyrights to of his books were now held by one publisher and, in lieu of earnings, Carman took what would ultimately be a disastrous financial stake in the company.

As the century turned Carman was hard at work on what would eventually be a five-volume set of poetry; "Pans Pipes". Pan, the goat-god, was traditionally associated with poetry and the coming together of the earthly and the divine. The five volumes were all published between 1902 – 1905.

The inspiration for this came from Mary who had persuaded Carman to write in both prose and poetry about the ideas of 'unitrinianism.' This drew on the theories of François-Alexandre-Nicolas-Chéri Delsarte and was defined as a strategy of mind-body-spirit harmonization aimed at undoing the physical, psychological, and spiritual damage caused by urban modernity. The definition may be rather woolly but for Carman it resulted in some very fine work across the five-volume series. This shared belief between Mary and Carman created a further bond but did isolate him from his circle of friends.

The excellence of a number of these poems did much to install Carman as the most noted of Canadian Poets and eventually their own Poet Laureate. Among the most often quoted and printed are "The Dead Faun" (from Volume I), "Lord of My Heart's Elation" (Volume II) and many of the erotic poems from Volume III.

In the middle of publication in 1903, Small, Maynard failed and with it went all the assets Carman had tied up in the company.

Carman immediately signed with another Boston publisher, L.C. Page, who would publish seven new books of Carman poetry in this hectic period up to 1905. They released a further three books based on Carman's Transcript columns, and a prose work on Unitrinianism, The Making of Personality, that he'd written with Mary King.

Carman now felt secure enough to pursue his 'dream project,' namely a deluxe edition of his collected poetry to 1903. Page acquired the distribution rights on the condition that the book be sold privately, by subscription. Unfortunately, the demand wasn't there and it failed. Carman was deeply disappointed and lost faith in Page. However, their grip on his copyrights was absolute and sadly no further collected editions were to be published during his lifetime.

By 1904 his income was restricted and the offer to be editor-in-chief of the 10-volume project, The World's Best Poetry, was eagerly accepted.

For Carman perhaps his best years as a poet were now behind him. From 1908 he lived near the Kings' New Canaan, Connecticut, estate, that he named "Sunshine", or in the summer in a cabin in the Catskills, which he called "Moonshine."

With Literary tastes now moving away from what he could provide his income further dwindled and his health started to deteriorate.

In 1912 Carman published the final work in the Vagabondia series. Richard Hovey had died in 1900 and so this last work was purely his. It has a distinct elegiac tone as if remembering the past works themselves.

Although Carman was not politically active he did campaign during the World War One, as a member of the Vigilantes, who supported the American entry into the titanic struggle on the Allied side.

By 1920, Carman was impoverished and recovering from a near-fatal attack of tuberculosis. He returned to Canada and began to undertake a series of publicly successful and somewhat lucrative reading tours, saying "there is nothing worth talking of in book sales compared with reading. Breathless attention, crowded halls, and a strange, profound enthusiasm such as I never guessed could be,' he reported to a friend. 'And good thrifty money too. Think of it! An entirely new life for me, and I am the most surprised person in Canada.'"

On October 28th, 1921 Carman was honored at a dinner held by the newly-formed Canadian Authors' Association, at the Ritz Carlton Hotel in Montreal, where he was crowned Canada's Poet Laureate with a wreath of maple leaves.

Carman is placed among the Confederation Poets, a group that included his cousin, Charles G.D. Roberts, Archibald Lampman, and Duncan Campbell Scott. Carman was perhaps the best and is credited with the widest recognition. However, whilst the others carefully supplemented their income with writing novels and works for the magazines, or even other careers, Carman only wrote poetry together with a small amount of writing on literary ideas, philosophy, and aesthetics.

He continued his reading tours, and by 1925 had finally secured a new Canadian publisher; McClelland & Stewart (Toronto), who issued a collection of selected earlier verse and would now became his main publisher. Although they benefited from Carman's increased popularity and his revered position in Canadian literature, his former publisher L.C. Page would not relinquish its copyrights to his earlier works.

In his last years, Carman was a member of the Halifax literary and social set, The Song Fishermen and in 1927 he edited The Oxford Book of American Verse.

William Bliss Carman died of a brain hemorrhage, at the age of 68, in New Canaan on the 8th June, 1929. He was cremated in New Canaan and his ashes interred at Forest Hill Cemetery, Fredericton, with a national memorial service held at the Anglican cathedral there.

It was only a quarter of a century later, on May 13th, 1954, that a scarlet maple tree was planted at his graveside, to honour his request in the 1892 poem "The Grave-Tree":

Let me have a scarlet maple
For the grave-tree at my head,
With the quiet sun behind it,
In the years when I am dead.

Bliss Carman – A Concise Bibliography

Poetry Collections
Low Tide on Grand Pre: A Book of Lyrics (1893)
Songs from Vagabondia (1894)
A Seamark: A Threnody for Robert Louis Stevenson (1895)
Behind the Arras: A Book of the Unseen (1895)
More Songs from Vagabondia (1896)
Ballads of Lost Haven: A Book of the Sea (1897)
By the Aurelian Wall: And Other Elegies (1898)
A Winter Holiday (1899)
Last Songs from Vagabondia (1901)

Ballads and Lyrics (1902)
Ode on the Coronation of King Edward (1902)
Pipes of Pan: From the Book of Myths (1902)
Pipes of Pan: From the Green Book of the Bards (1903)
Pipes of Pan: Songs of the Sea Children (1904)
Pipes of Pan: Songs from a Northern Garden (1904)
Pipes of Pan: From the Book of Valentines (1905)
Sappho: One Hundred Lyrics (1904)
Poems (1905)
The Rough Rider: And Other Poems (1909)
A Painter's Holiday, and Other Poems (1911)
Echoes from Vagabondia (1912)
April Airs: A Book of New England Lyrics (1916)
The Man of The Marne: And Other Poems (1918)
The Vengeance of Noel Brassard: A Tale of the Acadian Expulsion (1919)
Far Horizons (1925)
Later Poems (1926)
Sanctuary: Sunshine House Sonnets (1929)
Wild Garden (1929)
Bliss Carman's Poems (1931)

Drama

Bliss Carman & Mary Perry King. Daughters of Dawn: A Lyrical Pageant of a Series of Historical Scenes for Presentation with Music and Dancing (1913)
Bliss Carman & Mary Perry King. Earth Deities: And Other Rhythmic Masques (1914)

Prose Collections
The Kinship of Nature (1904)
The Poetry of Life (1905)
The Friendship of Art (1908)
The Making of Personality (1908)
Talks on Poetry and Life; Being a Series of Five Lectures Delivered Before the University of Toronto, December 1925 (Speech). transcribed by Blanche Hume. 1926.
Bliss Carman's Scrap-Book: A Table of Contents (Pierce, Lorne, editor) (1931)

Editor
The World's Best Poetry (10 volumes) (1904)
The Oxford Book of American Verse (U.S. editor) (1927)
Carman, Bliss; Pierce, Lorne, editors (1935). Our Canadian Literature: Representative Verse, English and French.